Editor
Sara Connolly

Illustrator
The Development Source

Cover Artist
Brenda DiAntonis

Editor in Chief
Ina Massler Levin, M.A.

Creative Director
Karen J. Goldfluss, M.S. Ed.

Art Production Manager
Kevin Barnes

Art Coordinator
Renée Christine Yates

Imaging
Craig Gunnell
Rosa C. See

Publisher
Mary D. Smith, M.S. Ed.

Grades 1-2

Activities FLUENCY

- Helps Build Confident Readers
- Improves Oral Reading Skills
- Introduces a Variety of Reading Materials

Author

Melissa Hart, M.F.A.

Teacher Created Resources, Inc.
12621 Western Avenue
Garden Grove, CA 92841
www.teachercreated.com
ISBN: 978-1-4206-8050-8

©2008 Teacher Created Resources, Inc.
Reprinted, 2022
Made in U.S.A.

Teacher Created Resources

Table of Contents

Introduction

A fluent child is an empowered child. Fluency implies much more than simply being able to read a piece of writing. Fluent students articulate with confidence; their words are clear and their voices are well-modulated. Fluent readers demonstrate not just reading skills but the ability to understand and make meaning of a written piece for both themselves and listeners.

Each section of *Activities for Fluency* has been designed with this goal in mind—-to create active, enthusiastic readers who know how to bring a piece of writing to life. In a 2002 interview with the former U.S. Assistant Secretary of the Office of Elementary and Secondary Education, Illinois reading expert Dr. Eunice Greer noted that fluency is the most neglected element of early reading instruction. "When kids can read rapidly and accurately," Dr. Greer explained, "what this does is this frees up their little brains so that they can attend to what the text is about, they can attend to meaning."

Activities for Fluency incorporates meaningful and exciting pieces across genres; it includes poetry, historical fiction, non-fiction, fables, readers' theater, and short stories. Teachers are encouraged to read each piece aloud, modeling skillful fluency techniques for students. In addition, students may read along with the teacher, copying pacing, tone, and inflection. Within each section, students explore vocabulary words and their meanings, and examine parts of speech and punctuation. They learn literary concepts such as figurative language, characterization and setting. They also learn to read aloud effectively, with emotion and inflection.

Each section of this book culminates in a Fluency Report Card which asks students to read a piece aloud to their teacher. The student receives feedback on key elements of fluency, including rate of reading, accuracy of word pronunciation, and tone. One part of the rubric allows teachers to note what students did best in their reading, whether in terms of poise and presentation, or simply in demonstrating the confidence to read an entire piece aloud.

As students move through grammar school to high school and college, they meet with countless opportunities to demonstrate fluency. Students are asked to read aloud in class, give speeches, participate in debates, and perform in plays. *Activities for Fluency* will help to develop skillful habits and techniques so that students can move through the educational system with self-assurance and success.

How to Use This Book

Activities for Fluency (Grades 1–2) offers students a variety of methods by which to become fluent, confident readers. Each section begins with a written piece: non-fiction, short fiction, scripts, songs, poems, and riddles. Activities follow, each designed to familiarize readers with unfamiliar words and punctuation marks in each piece. In addition, students will become familiar with stressed and unstressed syllables, breathing patterns in reading aloud, suffixes, prefixes, and root words, inflection, and reading with emotion. A fluency report card follows each section, designed to evaluate students' rate of reading, accuracy, and tone—that is, pitch, volume, and rhythm when reading aloud.

Read each piece aloud before beginning the accompanying activities. Then, ask students to read along with you, mimicking your own reading rate and tone. Next, invite students to complete the activities following each piece. These range from flash cards to picture and crossword puzzles, question and answer sections, word searches, bingo, and matching games. When you are confident that students can read a piece aloud fluently, evaluate them with the report card provided. A final section on the report card allows you to evaluate each student's particular strength in reading aloud.

As you work through the book, consider using these techniques:

- **Peer Readers**—Match a fluent reader up with a student whose skills are still developing. Ask each pair to work together, reading each piece aloud and completing the exercises.

- **Group Collaboration**—Many of these pieces are already in Readers' Theater format. Others are well-known songs or poems. Ask students to perform pieces in front of the class, to build familiarity with language, inflection, and characterization.

- **Bingo Cards**—Several sections of this book include Bingo cards. Consider mixing up cards from numerous pieces and using a variety of vocabulary words as students play.

- **Flash Cards**—Likewise, many sections of this book include flash cards with pictures on one side and words on the other. Consider cutting out flash cards and creating a master deck with which students can practice all of the vocabulary words in this book. They may use the cards to help memorize pronunciation and spelling, and they may also use them to form sentences.

How to Use This Book (cont.)

In addition, consider the following techniques for teaching vocabulary and fluency:

- Use a chosen word in five different sentences. Compare sentences and discuss.

- Write a short story using as many of the words as possible. Students may then read their stories in groups.

- Encourage your students to use each new vocabulary word in a conversation five times during one day. They can take notes on how and when the word was used, and then share their experience with the class.

- Play "Vocabulary Charades." Each student or group of students gets a word to act out. Other students must guess the word.

- Play "Vocabulary Pictures." Each student or group of students must draw a picture representing a word on the chalkboard or on paper. Other students must guess the word.

- Challenge students to a Vocabulary Bee. In groups or separately, students must spell the word correctly and give its proper definition.

- Write the words with glue on stiff paper, and then cover the glue with glitter or sand. Alternatively, students may write the words with a squeeze bottle full of jam on bread to create an edible lesson!

- Write a class play using as many vocabulary words as possible. Read the play as a class, and have students call out each vocabulary word as they come to it.

- Ask students to write a song using as many vocabulary words as possible. Sing the song as a class and have students clap every time they come to a vocabulary word.

- Assign each student a word and provide magazines and newspapers, along with paper, scissors, and glue. Then, make a collage to show different interpretations of one vocabulary word.

Fluency is much more than reading a piece without mistakes. We hope that this book will encourage your students to personalize their reading through thoughtful pacing, inventive performance techniques, and creative methods of making each piece of writing their own.

Standards

Each lesson in *Activities for Fluency* (Grades 1–2) meets one or more of the following standards, which are used with permission from McREL (Copyright 2007, McREL, Mid-continent Research for Education and Learning. Telephone: 303/337-0990. Website: www.mcrel.org.)

Language Arts Standards	Page Number
Writes in a variety of forms or genres for different purposes; uses descriptive words to convey basic ideas	77
Uses grammatical and mechanical conventions in written compositions	58-60, 67, 68, 76, 93, 121, 133
Uses mental images based on pictures and print to aid in comprehension of text	8, 16, 32, 37, 52, 64, 65, 88, 88, 96, 18
Uses a picture dictionary to determine word meaning	8, 9, 16-20, 25, 32, 49, 50, 61, 64, 65, 73, 80, 88-92, 96, 115-116, 122-125, 128
Uses basic elements of structural analysis to decode unknown words	24, 27-29, 40-45, 51, 56, 117, 131, 132
Understands level-appropriate sight words and vocabulary	11, 12, 33, 34, 69, 100, 99, 104, 106, 112, 114, 120
Reads aloud familiar stories, poems, and passages with fluency and expression	7, 14, 15, 22, 23, 30, 31, 38, 39, 46, 47, 54, 55, 62, 63, 70, 71, 78, 79, 86, 87, 94, 95, 102, 103, 110, 11, 118, 119, 126, 127, 134-136
Uses reading skills and strategies to understand a variety of familiar literary passages and texts	7, 15, 23, 31, 38, 46, 54, 63, 71, 71, 79, 87, 95, 103, 111, 119, 127
Knows setting, main characters, main events, sequence, and problems in stories; summarizes information found in texts	13, 21, 53, 57, 66, 81, 105, 113
Uses different voice levels, phrasing, and intonation for different situations	35, 36, 82-84, 109
Recites and responds to familiar stories, poems, and rhymes with patterns	85, 107, 108, 130

Sam and the Ball

Sam was a dog. He was big and brown. He loved to play with a green ball.

One day, Sam lost his ball. He was sad.

He found a toy in the kitchen. "No. That is an egg, Sam," said the girl.

Sam found a toy in the bedroom. "No. That is a shoe, Sam," said the boy.

Then they gave him a new green ball. Sam played and played. Now he was happy.

Picture Words

Directions: Study the words beside the pictures. Say them out loud with your teacher. Then, say them out loud by yourself.

dog		ball	
kitchen		egg	
girl		bedroom	
shoe		boy	

8

Flash Cards

Note to Teacher: Make double-sided copies, aligning words with the correct pictures so that they appear front-to-back.

Directions: Cut out these flash cards on the lines. Use them to practice fluency before reading "Sam and the Ball" on page 7.

ball	dog
egg	kitchen
bedroom	girl
boy	shoe

Flash Cards *(cont.)*

10

Color the Story

Directions: Follow the instructions below to color pictures from the story.

1. Color the dog brown.

2. Color the ball green.

3. Color the egg blue.

4. Color the shoe black.

Write the Word

Directions: Write the word below the picture.

Fill in the Blanks

Directions: Look at the story of Sam and the Ball, below. Fill in the blanks with the correct words.

Sam and the Ball

Sam was a _____ . He was big and brown. He loved

to play with a _____ ball.

One day, Sam lost his ball. He was sad.

He found a toy in the kitchen. "No. That is an egg, Sam," said

the _____ .

Sam found a toy in the bedroom. "No.

That is a _____, Sam," said the boy.

Then they gave him a new green _____ . Sam played

and _____ . Now he was happy.

Fluency Report Card

Directions: Read the story out loud to your teacher. Ask your teacher to time your reading with a watch.

Together, fill out the chart below.

Rate of Reading	Minutes Seconds
Accuracy	Number of Mistakes
Tone	Pitch, Volume, and Rhythm
What You Did Best	Your strengths in fluency!

*Note to Teacher

Rate of Reading: Student should read at a pleasant, conversational pace, not too slowly, and not too quickly.

Accuracy: Student should read with a minimum of mistakes in pronunciation and pauses for punctuation.

Tone: Student should read at a pleasant pitch, with moderate volume, and should vary rhythm as appropriate to each sentence.

The Boat Ride

Meg liked boats. She liked to watch them on the lake. She liked to draw them on paper.

Father told Meg that he would take her on a boat ride. "Let us wait until the wind is gone," he said.

"I want to go for a ride now," Meg said.

They got into a small boat. The wind grew stronger.

It made big waves. Meg felt sick. Father held her hand.

At last, they got back to the land. Father and Meg stepped off the boat. "Next time, I will wait until the wind is gone," she said.

Picture Words

Directions: Study the words beside the pictures. Say them out loud with your teacher. Then, say them out loud by yourself.

boat		lake	
paper		waves	
Meg		Father	
land		hand	

Word Bingo

Directions: Play Bingo, using words from "The Boat Ride."

Copy the words below onto individual file cards or small pieces of paper. Choose one person to be the Caller. The Caller begins by choosing one word to call out. Each player then marks the square on his or her game card which contains that word.

Players may use markers in the form of dried beans, pennies, or small pebbles. You may want to play so that the first person to mark off an entire row across, down, or diagonally wins. Alternatively, you might want to play until every word has been called and marked.

boat	wind	Father
lake	waves	paper
Meg	hand	land

Word Bingo *(cont.)*

waves	Meg	hand
paper	boat	lake
wind	Father	land

18

Word Bingo *(cont.)*

land	lake	Father
wind	boat	Meg
paper	hand	waves

Word Bingo *(cont.)*

Father	lake	land
waves	Meg	wind
hand	paper	boat

The Boat Ride

Which Word?

Directions: Below, circle the correct word in each pair to complete the sentence. Then, write the word in the blank.

1. _____ likes to draw boats. Father   Meg

2. Meg rides a boat on the _____. lake   land

3. The _____ makes big waves. paper   wind

4. Meg feels _____ on the boat. sick   lake

5. "I want to go for a _____ now." gone   ride

Fluency Report Card

Directions: Read the story out loud to your teacher. Ask your teacher to time your reading with a watch.

Together, fill out the chart below.

Rate of Reading	Minutes Seconds
Accuracy	Number of Mistakes
Tone	Pitch, Volume, and Rhythm
What You Did Best	Your strengths in fluency!

*Note to Teacher

Rate of Reading: Student should read at a pleasant, conversational pace, not too slowly, and not too quickly.

Accuracy: Student should read with a minimum of mistakes in pronunciation and pauses for punctuation.

Tone: Student should read at a pleasant pitch, with moderate volume, and should vary rhythm as appropriate to each sentence.

Yankee Doodle

British soldiers wrote this tune to tease American soldiers.

Yankee Doodle came to town,

riding on a pony.

He stuck a feather in his hat

and called it macaroni.

Yankee Doodle keep it up!

Yankee Doodle Dandy!

Mind the music and the steps,

and with the girls be handy.

Flash Cards

Note to Teacher: Make double-sided copies, aligning words with the correct pictures so that they appear front-to-back.

Directions: Cut out these flash cards on the lines. Use them to practice fluency before reading "Yankee Doodle."

pony	town
hat	feather
up	macaroni
steps	music

Flash Cards (cont.)

Syllables

A syllable is one unit of spoken language. Some words have just one syllable, such as "to" or "on." Other words have two syllables, such as "pony" or "music." Some words have three or four syllables, such as "macaroni."

Directions: Study the words below. Count how many syllables are in each word. Write the correct number in the space provided.

The first one has been done for you.

Word	Number of Syllables
1. Doodle	2
2. town	
3. feather	
4. stuck	
5. hat	
6. handy	

Stressed and Unstressed Syllables

Syllables are either stressed or unstressed. This gives spoken language its rhythm. You can tell which syllables are stressed and unstressed by clapping as you sing or recite a song.

Directions: Sing Yankee Doodle, below. Stressed syllables have a "\" symbol over them. Unstressed syllables have a "−" symbol over them. Recite the poem. Clap along, clapping loudly with stressed syllables, and very softly with unstressed syllables.

\ − \ − \ − \
Yankee Doodle came to town,

\ − \ - \ −
riding on a pony.

− \ - \ − \ − \
He stuck a feather in his hat

− \ − \ − \ −
and called it macaroni.

\ − \ − \ − \
Yankee Doodle keep it up!

\ − \ − \ −
Yankee Doodle Dandy!

\ − \ − \ − \
Mind the music and the steps,

− \ − \ − \ −
and with the girls be handy.

Stressed Syllables

Directions: Study the words below. First, they appear complete. Then, they are broken up into syllables. Circle the stressed syllables. The first one has been done for you.

1. Yankee   (Yan) - kee

2. handy   han - dy

3. music   mu - sic

4. riding   ri - ding

5. feather   fea - ther

Unstressed Syllables

Directions: Study the words below. First, they appear complete. Then, they are broken up into syllables. Circle the unstressed syllables. The first one has been done for you.

1. Doodle   Doo - (dle)

2. pony   po - ny

3. dandy   dan - dy

4. Yankee   Yan - kee

5. macaroni   ma - ca - ro - ni

Fluency Report Card

Directions: Read the story out loud to your teacher. Ask your teacher to time your reading with a watch.

Together, fill out the chart below.

Rate of Reading	Minutes Seconds
Accuracy	Number of Mistakes
Tone	Pitch, Volume, and Rhythm
What You Did Best	Your strengths in fluency!

*****Note to Teacher**

Rate of Reading: Student should read at a pleasant, conversational pace, not too slowly, and not too quickly.

Accuracy: Student should read with a minimum of mistakes in pronunciation and pauses for punctuation.

Tone: Student should read at a pleasant pitch, with moderate volume, and should vary rhythm as appropriate to each sentence.

This Land Is Your Land

Woodie Guthrie wrote this song to celebrate the United States.

This land is your land,

This land is my land

From California

To the New York Island,

From the redwood forest,

To the Gulf stream waters,

This land was made for you and me!

As I was walking,

That ribbon of highway,

I saw above me

That endless skyway,

I saw below me

That golden valley.

This land was made for you and me.

Picture Words

Directions: Study the words beside the pictures. Say them out loud with your teacher. Then, say them out loud by yourself.

land	ribbon
highway	sky
island	redwood
forest	valley

Color the Words

Directions: Color the picture according to the instructions below it.

1. Color the island green.

2. Color the sky blue.

3. Color the forest brown.

4. Color the valley yellow.

5. Color the highway black.

Land Maze

Directions: Help the children travel from California to New York. Write in the correct word under or beside each picture. Use the words from the Word Bank below.

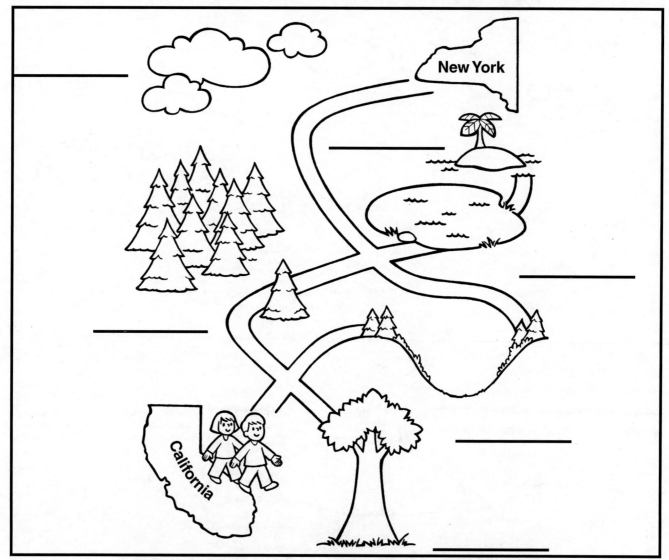

Word Bank	
forest	redwood
water	island
sky	valley

34

Breathing

Good readers know when to take a breath as they read out loud. Try not to take a breath in the middle of a phrase. Instead, take a breath when you see a period or come to the end of a thought. This helps your reading to flow smoothly.

Directions: Below, read "This Land Is Your Land." Take a breath when you see a smiley face.

 This land is your land,

This land is my land

From California,

To the New York Island

From the redwood forest,

To the Gulf stream waters

This land was made for you and me!

As I was walking

That ribbon of highway

I saw above me

That endless skyway

I saw below me

That golden valley

This land was made for you and me!

More on Breathing

Directions: Read the sentences below out loud. Draw a smiley face wherever you feel you should take a breath. Remember not to breathe in the middle of a phrase! The first one is done for you.

1. I was walking in the forest one day, when I saw a little dog.

2. He sat in a golden valley, and he looked lost and sad.

3. I called to the dog to come to me, but he just sat still.

4. "Spot!" I said. Then, the dog ran to me and barked.

5. Now, a little girl walked up. "There you are, Spot!" she said.

6. The dog jumped up on the girl and licked her face. "I thought he was lost," she told me.

Our Land

Directions: Fill in the blanks below using words from the Word Bank. Choose the best word for each sentence.

1. We drive our cars on the _____ .

2. The _____ has many trees.

3. The _____ has water all around it.

4. She lives down in the _____ near the forest.

5. I like to swim in the _____ by my house.

6. The _____ has white clouds today.

Word Bank	
forest	highway
water	sky
island	valley

Fluency Report Card

Directions: Read the story out loud to your teacher. Ask your teacher to time your reading with a watch.

Together, fill out the chart below.

Rate of Reading	Minutes Seconds
Accuracy	Number of Mistakes
Tone	Pitch, Volume, and Rhythm
What You Did Best	Your strengths in fluency!

*Note to Teacher

Rate of Reading: Student should read at a pleasant, conversational pace, not too slowly, and not too quickly.

Accuracy: Student should read with a minimum of mistakes in pronunciation and pauses for punctuation.

Tone: Student should read at a pleasant pitch, with moderate volume, and should vary rhythm as appropriate to each sentence.

Owning a Rabbit

Rabbits make good pets. They are friendly. They are playful.

Your rabbit can live in the house. Give it a toy to chew. That way, it will not chew cords or chairs.

Rabbits are furry and nice to touch. Brush your rabbit softly. You will want to clip its claws, too.

Give your rabbit a box filled with straw. Make sure to offer water, hay, and carrots. This will keep your rabbit happy and healthy!

Root Words

A root word is like a building block. You can add a prefix or a suffix to make a new word.

Directions: Below, study the root words from "Owning a Rabbit." Say each word out loud. Then, copy it in the space given.

own

soft

friend

health

play

40

The Suffix

A suffix is a group of letters that you put on the end of a root word. This turns the root word into a different word.

Directions: Study the root words and the suffixes below. Then, write the root and the suffix as one word in the space provided.

Root Word	Suffix	New Word
1. own	+ ing	= _____
2. friend	+ ly	= _____
3. play	+ ful	= _____
4. soft	+ ly	= _____
5. health	+ y	= _____

Many Words

Directions: Look at the list of root words below. Then, look at the list of suffixes. You can make twelve new words by combining root words and suffixes! Write your new words in the Word Bank below. The first one has been done for you.

Root Word
health
soft
play
own
friend

Suffix
ly
er
ful
ed
ing
y

Word Bank

playing

_____   _____   _____

_____   _____   _____

_____   _____   _____

New Nouns

A noun is a person, place, or thing.

Directions: Study the nouns beside the pictures. Say them out loud with your teacher. Then, say them out loud by yourself.

rabbit		house	
toy		cord	
chair		box	
water		carrot	

Writing Nouns

Directions: Study the pictures below. Then, write the correct noun next to each picture.

Picture	Noun

Building Sentences

You can build new sentences from words in "Owning a Rabbit."

Directions: Study the nouns below. Then, study the root words and suffixes. Combine each root word with a suffix. Choose a noun or nouns from the first box and root-suffix combinations from the second and third boxes to create five new sentences on the lines given.

Nouns
rabbit
chair
house
water
carrot

Root Word
own
play
soft
health
friend

Suffixes
ed
er
ing
s
ly

Example: _He owned a house._

1. _____

2. _____

3. _____

4. _____

5. _____

Fluency Report Card

Directions: Read the story out loud to your teacher. Ask your teacher to time your reading with a watch.

Together, fill out the chart below.

Rate of Reading	Minutes Seconds
Accuracy	Number of Mistakes
Tone	Pitch, Volume, and Rhythm
What You Did Best	Your strengths in fluency!

*Note to Teacher

Rate of Reading: Student should read at a pleasant, conversational pace, not too slowly, and not too quickly.

Accuracy: Student should read with a minimum of mistakes in pronunciation and pauses for punctuation.

Tone: Student should read at a pleasant pitch, with moderate volume, and should vary rhythm as appropriate to each sentence.

Why We Love Trees

A tree is a plant. It has a trunk and leaves. It has branches and twigs. Trees have roots underground.

Trees replace bad air with good air. People need air to breathe. This is one reason to love trees.

Trees also give us shade. It is nice to sit beside a tree in the sun. Trees keep us cool.

Some trees give us fruit. People pick it off trees. Trees transform our world.

It is good to plant a tree. Find some land. Dig a hole. Cover the tree roots with dirt. Discover the joy of trees!

Prefixes

A prefix is a group of letters that you put at the beginning of a root word. This turns the root word into a different word.

Directions: Study the prefixes and the root words below. Then, write the prefix and root word as one word in the spaces provided.

Prefix	Root Word	New Word
1. be	+ side	= _____
2. dis	+ cover	= _____
3. under	+ ground	= _____
4. re	+ place	= _____
5. trans	+ form	= _____

Fill in the Blanks

Directions: Look at the article titled "Why We Love Trees" below. Fill in the blanks by writing the correct words from the Word Bank below.

Why We Love Trees

A tree is a plant. It has a trunk and leaves. It has branches and twigs. Trees have roots _____.

Trees _____ bad air with good air. People need air to breathe. This is one reason to love trees.

Trees also give us shade. It is nice to sit _____ a tree in the sun. Trees keep us cool.

Some trees give us fruit. People pick it off trees. Trees _____ our world.

It is good to plant a tree. Find some land. Dig a hole. Cover the tree roots with dirt. _____ the joy of trees!

Word Bank	
transform	discover
replace	beside
underground	

Parts of a Tree

Directions: Study the parts of a tree below. Write the correct part on each line. Then, color the tree.

Flash Cards

Note to Teacher: Make double-sided copies, aligning words with the correct pictures so that they appear front-to-back.

Directions: Cut out these flash cards on the lines. Use them to practice fluency before reading "Why We Love Trees."

people	tree
fruit	sun
land	hole
branches	dirt

Flash Cards *(cont.)*

52

Why We Love Trees

Which Word?

Directions: Circle the word that best completes each sentence. The first one has been done for you.

1. You can find _____ underground.   leaves   (roots)

2. You might _____ apples on a tree!   discover   replace

3. Have a picnic _____ a tree.   beside   transform

4. Trees _____ their leaves each year.   discover   replace

5. A _____ makes air for us to breathe.   trunk   tree

©*Teacher Created Resources, Inc.*   53   *#8050 Activities for Fluency*

Fluency Report Card

Directions: Read the story out loud to your teacher. Ask your teacher to time your reading with a watch.

Together, fill out the chart below.

Rate of Reading	Minutes Seconds	
Accuracy	Number of Mistakes	
Tone	Pitch, Volume, and Rhythm	
What You Did Best	Your strengths in fluency!	

*Note to Teacher

Rate of Reading: Student should read at a pleasant, conversational pace, not too slowly, and not too quickly.

Accuracy: Student should read with a minimum of mistakes in pronunciation and pauses for punctuation.

Tone: Student should read at a pleasant pitch, with moderate volume, and should vary rhythm as appropriate to each sentence.

54

Jack Sprat

This is a classic nursery rhyme written long ago about King Charles I and his wife.

Jack Sprat could eat no fat.

His wife could eat no lean.

And so between the two of them,

They licked the platter clean.

Jack ate all the lean.

The queen ate all the fat.

The bone they chewed it clean,

Then threw it to the cat.

Nouns and Verbs

A verb is an action word. It shows what someone is doing.

Directions: Study the nouns and verbs beside the pictures. Say them out loud with your teacher. Then, say the nouns and verbs out loud by yourself.

Nouns		Verbs	
Jack		eat	
platter		licked	
queen		chewed	
cat		threw	

56

Present and Past

In "Jack Sprat," verbs are written in the present or past tense.

Directions: Study the chart. Then, study the sentences below. Circle the correct form of the verb and write it in the blank.

Present Tense	Past Tense
eat	ate
lick	licked
chew	chewed
throw	threw

1. Yesterday, the queen _____ meat.

   eat ate

2. Jack _____ a bone, and the cat eats it.

   threw throws

3. " _____ that bone, Jack," said the queen.

   Chew Chewed

4. The cat _____ the platter.

   licked lick

5. You should _____ your food.

   chewed chew

Word Search

Directions: Study the six words in the Word Bank. Circle them in the Word Search below.

A	D	F	K	G	L	E
P	L	A	T	T	E	R
W	Q	M	W	Z	E	P
Q	S	B	C	A	A	Y
U	D	E	B	L	T	U
E	C	B	O	N	E	C
E	J	A	N	X	K	S
N	L	I	C	K	E	D
C	A	T	H	C	P	G

Word Bank	
eat	queen
bone	cat
licked	platter

Periods

Directions: A period shows that you should stop for a moment at the end of a sentence before you continue reading. It looks like this ___·___ .

There are six periods missing from the poem below. Draw a period at the end of each sentence to show where you should stop for a moment when reading this poem out loud.

Jack Sprat

Jack Sprat could eat no fat

His wife could eat no lean

And so between the two of them,

They licked the platter clean

Jack ate all the lean

The queen ate all the fat

The bone they chewed it clean,

Then threw it to the cat

59

Flash Cards

Note to Teacher: Make double-sided copies, aligning words with the correct pictures so that they appear front-to-back.

Directions: Cut out these flash cards on the lines. Use them to create sentences which end in a period.

cat	queen
Jack	ate
threw	platter
the	bone
a	.

Flash Cards (cont.)

Fluency Report Card

Directions: Read the story out loud to your teacher. Ask your teacher to time your reading with a watch.

Together, fill out the chart below.

Rate of Reading	Minutes Seconds
Accuracy	Number of Mistakes
Tone	Pitch, Volume, and Rhythm
What You Did Best	Your strengths in fluency!

*Note to Teacher

Rate of Reading: Student should read at a pleasant, conversational pace, not too slowly, and not too quickly.

Accuracy: Student should read with a minimum of mistakes in pronunciation and pauses for punctuation.

Tone: Student should read at a pleasant pitch, with moderate volume, and should vary rhythm as appropriate to each sentence.

Saint Ives

This is a nonsense poem in the form of a riddle.

As I was going to Saint Ives,

I met a man with seven wives.

Each wife had seven sacks,

Each sack had seven cats,

Each cat had seven kits.

Kits, cats, sacks, and wives,

How many were going to Saint Ives?

(The answer to the riddle—only one!)

Picture Cards

Directions: Study the words on the picture cards below. Say them out loud with your teacher. Then, read them out loud by yourself.

man	wife
sack	cat
seven	kit
I	walk

Picture Words

Directions: Study the pictures below. Then, write the correct word underneath each picture. You may use the words in the Word Bank at the bottom of this page.

Word Bank	
sack	man
kit	cat
wife	walk
I	seven

How Many?

Directions: Study the words on the left. Draw a picture in each box on the right to illustrate the words. Then, count your pictures.

a man	
seven wives	
seven cats	
seven kits	

How many pictures did you draw? _____

Commas

A comma shows that you should pause for a moment in the middle of a sentence before you continue reading. It looks like this __,__ .

Directions: There are seven commas missing from the poem below. Put in the commas to show where you should pause for a moment when reading this poem out loud.

Saint Ives

As I was going to Saint Ives

I met a man with seven wives.

Each wife had seven sacks

Each sack had seven cats

Each cat had seven kits.

Kits cats sacks and wives

How many were going to Saint Ives?

Commas in Action

Directions: Fill in the blanks with words from the Word Bank below. (Some words are used more than once.) Use commas where you need to show a pause in the sentence.

When you are finished, read the sentences out loud.

1. The man his _____ and his _____ went to Saint Ives.

2. I put the _____ in a _____ called to my _____ and went for a _____ .

3. _____ walked _____ days then found my lost _____ .

4. My _____ pets her _____ but it bites.

5. The _____ the _____ and the _____ took a _____ .

Word Bank	
I	man
wife	cat
sack	seven
walk	

Crossword

Directions: Answer the questions by writing in words from the Word Bank on the spaces below. Then, fill in the crossword.

Across

3. Her _____ had baby kits.

5. His _____ owns seven cats.

6. The _____ could not find his sack.

Down

1. The man and his wife went for a _____ .

2. Each wife had _____ cats.

4. I put my bone in an empty _____ .

Word Bank	
cats	wife
walk	man
sack	seven

Fluency Report Card

Directions: Read the story out loud to your teacher. Ask your teacher to time your reading with a watch.

Together, fill out the chart below.

Rate of Reading	Minutes Seconds
Accuracy	Number of Mistakes
Tone	Pitch, Volume, and Rhythm
What You Did Best	Your strengths in fluency!

*Note to Teacher

Rate of Reading: Student should read at a pleasant, conversational pace, not too slowly, and not too quickly.

Accuracy: Student should read with a minimum of mistakes in pronunciation and pauses for punctuation.

Tone: Student should read at a pleasant pitch, with moderate volume, and should vary rhythm as appropriate to each sentence.

The Rat

March 2, 2007

Dear Jo,

How are you? I am well. Today, I got a new rat. It is white. It is very nice.

Do you still own a horse? I own a horse, a cow, and the new rat. I play with them after school.

Do you like school? I like school a lot. I have a friend named Sal. He likes rats, too.

Write back soon.

Your friend,

Tom

Flash Cards

Note to Teacher: Make double-sided copies, aligning words with the correct pictures so that they appear front-to-back.

Directions: Cut out these flash cards on the lines. Use them to practice fluency before reading "The Rat" for your Fluency Report Card.

school	you
friend	rat
write	horse
play	cow

Flash Cards (cont.)

Which Word?

Directions: Study the sentences below. Select the best word to fill in each blank. Write the correct word on the blank.

1. Today, I got a new pet _____ .   school   cow

2. How are _____ ?   I   you

3. I like to _____ ball.   play   rat

4. Sal rides a _____ .   rat   horse

5. _____ back soon.   Write   Friend

Parts of a Letter

A letter has several parts. It has a date. It has a greeting. It has names. It has a closing.

Directions: Study the letter below. It is missing five parts. Look at the clues under each blank line. Using the Word Bank at the bottom of the page, choose one date, one greeting, two names, and one closing. Write them on the blank lines.

_____
      (date)

_____ _____,
   (greeting)   (name)

How are you? I am well. Today, I got a new rat. It is white. It is very nice.

Do you still own a horse? I own a horse, a cow, and the new rat. I play with them after school.

Do you like school? I like school a lot. I have a friend named Sal. He likes rats, too.

Write back soon.

_____,
     (closing)

_____
     (name)

Dates
March 2, 2007
July 4, 2008
January 1, 2009

Greetings
Dear
Hello
Good day

Closings
Your Friend
From
Love

Names
Meg
Tom
Sam

Question Marks

A question mark at the end of a sentence shows readers that you are asking a question. It looks like this: ___?___ .

Directions: Study the sentences below. Some need a question mark. Some need a period. Write the correct form of punctuation in the space after the sentence. The first one has been done for you.

1. He likes rats _____.

2. How are you _____

3. The rat is white _____

4. Do you like cows _____

5. Who likes school _____

6. Jo owns a horse _____

Write Your Own Letter

Directions: Write your own letter in the space below. Don't forget a date, a greeting, names, and a closing!

When you have finished your letter, read it out loud to your class.

Fluency Report Card

Directions: Read the story out loud to your teacher. Ask your teacher to time your reading with a watch.

Together, fill out the chart below.

Rate of Reading	Minutes Seconds
Accuracy	Number of Mistakes
Tone	Pitch, Volume, and Rhythm
What You Did Best	Your strengths in fluency!

*Note to Teacher

Rate of Reading: Student should read at a pleasant, conversational pace, not too slowly, and not too quickly.

Accuracy: Student should read with a minimum of mistakes in pronunciation and pauses for punctuation.

Tone: Student should read at a pleasant pitch, with moderate volume, and should vary rhythm as appropriate to each sentence.

The Lost Dollar

Dad gave Tara a dollar. She showed it to Katy. She showed it to Bill. Then, she lost it.

"Did you take my dollar?" Tara asked Katy.

Katy shook her head. "I did not take your dollar," she said.

Tara walked up to Bill. "Did you take my dollar?" she asked.

Bill smiled. "What is that on your shoe?"

Tara looked down at her shoe. There was her dollar, stuck to the bottom. "I am sorry," she told her friends. "I will buy us all some candy."

Words and Pictures

Directions: Study the words in the left column. Study the pictures in the right column. Then, draw a line from each word to the correct picture.

shoe

friends

dollar

head

smile

candy

Dad

Questions

Directions: Answer the questions about "The Lost Dollar" below. You may use the words in the Word Bank if you need help.

1. Who gives Tara a dollar?

   _____

2. Who does Tara show her dollar to?

   _____

3. Who are Bill and Katy?

   _____

4. What does Tara have on her shoe?

   _____

5. What does Tara say to her friends?

   _____

Word Bank	
I'm sorry.	a dollar
friends	Bill and Katy
Dad	

Inflection

Inflection means the way in which you change your voice as you read. You should stress key words in each sentence.

Directions: Below, read each sentence. Put a stress on the word that is underlined. See how the sentence changes when you stress one particular word.

<u>I</u> did not take your dollar.   (Someone else might have!)

I <u>did</u> not take your dollar.   (Shows anger.)

I did <u>not</u> take your dollar.   (Shows even more anger.)

I did not <u>take</u> your dollar.   (Maybe I borrowed it . . .)

I did not take <u>your</u> dollar.   (I may have taken someone else's)

I did not take your <u>dollar</u>.   (But I might have taken something else belonging to you!)

Robot Reading

One of the best ways to learn proper inflection is to read incorrectly. Break into groups of three. Each of you can take a turn reading "The Lost Dollar" below like a robot.

Directions: Read in an even, steady tone. Don't let your voice get higher or lower. How does this story sound when you read like a robot? How does inflection change the story?

Dad gave Tara a dollar. She showed it to Katy. She showed it to Bill. Then, she lost it.

"Did you take my dollar?" Tara asked Katy.

Katy shook her head. "I did not take your dollar," she said.

Tara walked up to Bill. "Did you take my dollar?" she asked.

Bill smiled. "What is that on your shoe?"

Tara looked down at her shoe. There was her dollar, stuck to the bottom. "I am sorry," she told her friends. "I will buy us all some candy."

Emotional Reading

Tara thinks her friends have taken her dollar. How would you feel if someone accused you of stealing?

Tara's question and Katy's and Bill's responses are below.

Directions: Read each out loud with different emotions, according to the suggestions in parenthesis.

Tara's Question

Did you take my dollar? (Angry)

Did you take my dollar? (Sad)

Did you take my dollar? (Scared)

Did you take my dollar? (Amused)

Katy's and Bill's Responses

I did not take your dollar. (Scared)

I did not take your dollar. (Amused)

I did not take your dollar. (Angry)

I did not take your dollar. (Sad)

Readers' Theater

Directions: You can read "The Lost Dollar" like a play. Choose one person to be Tara. Choose one person to be Bill. Choose one person to be Katy. Choose one person to be the narrator. Then, act out the play below using inflection.

The Lost Dollar

Narrator: Dad gave Tara a dollar. She showed it to Katy. She showed it to Bill. Then, she lost it.

Tara: Did you take my dollar?

Narrator: Katy shook her head.

Katy: I did not take your dollar.

Narrator: Tara walked up to Bill.

Tara: Did you take my dollar?

Narrator: Bill smiled.

Bill: What is that on your shoe?

Narrator: Tara looked down at her shoe. There was her dollar, stuck to the bottom.

Tara: I am sorry. I will buy us all some candy.

Narrator: The End

Fluency Report Card

Directions: Read the story out loud to your teacher. Ask your teacher to time your reading with a watch.

Together, fill out the chart below.

Rate of Reading	Minutes Seconds
Accuracy	Number of Mistakes
Tone	Pitch, Volume, and Rhythm
What You Did Best	Your strengths in fluency!

*Note to Teacher

Rate of Reading: Student should read at a pleasant, conversational pace, not too slowly, and not too quickly.

Accuracy: Student should read with a minimum of mistakes in pronunciation and pauses for punctuation.

Tone: Student should read at a pleasant pitch, with moderate volume, and should vary rhythm as appropriate to each sentence.

Kookaburra

The Kookaburra is a bird native to Australia. Sound out the syllables to pronounce its name. Kook-a-bur-ra.

You may want to read this song first, and then sing it.

Kookaburra sits in the old gum tree.

Merry, merry king of the bush is he.

Laugh, Kookaburra!

Laugh, Kookaburra!

Fun your life must be.

Kookaburra sits in the old gum tree,

Eating all the gumdrops he can see.

Stop, Kookaburra!

Stop, Kookaburra!

Leave some there for me.

Picture Words

Directions: Study the words beside the pictures. Say them out loud with your teacher. Then, say them out loud by yourself.

sit		tree	
see		king	
laugh		eat	
gumdrop		stop	

bush	

Word Bingo

Directions: Play Bingo, using words from "Kookaburra."

Copy the words below onto individual file cards or small pieces of paper. Choose one person to be the Caller. The Caller begins by choosing one word to call out. Each player then marks the square on his or her game card which contains that word.

Players may use markers in the form of dried beans, pennies, or small pebbles. You may want to play so that the first person to mark off an entire row across, down, or diagonally wins. Alternatively, you might want to play until every word has been called and marked.

Word Bingo *(cont.)*

stop	laugh	sit
king	see	bush
gumdrop	eat	tree

Word Bingo *(cont.)*

laugh	see	eat
bush	stop	king
tree	sit	gumdrop

Word Bingo *(cont.)*

sit	eat	tree
king	gumdrop	bush
see	laugh	stop

Exclamation Points

An exclamation point at the end of a sentence shows readers that you are exclaiming over something with enthusiasm. It looks like this: __!__ .

Directions: Study the sentences below. Some need an exclamation point. Some need a question mark. Write the correct form of punctuation in the space after the sentence. The first one has been done for you.

1. Laugh, Kookaburra   __!__

2. Where is the tree   _____

3. Stop eating so much   _____

4. Who likes gumdrops   _____

5. Look at that bird   _____

Fluency Report Card

Directions: Read the story out loud to your teacher. Ask your teacher to time your reading with a watch.

Together, fill out the chart below.

Rate of Reading	Minutes Seconds
Accuracy	Number of Mistakes
Tone	Pitch, Volume, and Rhythm
What You Did Best	Your strengths in fluency!

*Note to Teacher

Rate of Reading: Student should read at a pleasant, conversational pace, not too slowly, and not too quickly.

Accuracy: Student should read with a minimum of mistakes in pronunciation and pauses for punctuation.

Tone: Student should read at a pleasant pitch, with moderate volume, and should vary rhythm as appropriate to each sentence.

How to Play Soccer

Soccer is a fun game. Many kids like to play it. You must run and kick a ball.

There are two teams in soccer. Each team has eleven players. Soccer is played on the grass. There is a goal at each end of the grass.

Players try to kick the ball into the other team's goal. The other team tries to stop them.

Soccer is called "football" in most places. It is played all over the world!

Flash Cards

Note to Teacher: Make double-sided copies, aligning words with the correct pictures so that they appear front-to-back.

Directions: Cut out these flash cards on the lines. Use them to practice fluency before reading "How to Play Soccer."

run	kid
two	kick
grass	goal
world	soccer

Flash Cards *(cont.)*

Color the Picture

Directions: Color the picture, following the instructions below.

1. Color the grass green.

2. Color the soccer ball black.

3. Color the kid blue.

4. Color the two yellow.

5. Color the goal red.

Word Soccer

Directions: Count off so that you have two teams. On a chalk or dry-erase board, draw a picture of two soccer goals—one on either side of the board.

- Ask students to form two lines. Read (or have a student read) one of the vocabulary words out loud. Then, the first student on each team will run up to the board and attempt to write the word correctly under or beside the other team's goal.

- The first student to write the word correctly earns a point for his or her team. Repeat with the second student in each line, and a new vocabulary word.

- Alternatively, the reader can call out the definition, and the student can simply write the answer.

- Congratulate and reward both teams for playing well and learning new words to increase their fluency!

Word Search

Directions: Find eight words from "How to Play Soccer" in the Word Search below.

W	E	E	T	C	G	Y
R	U	N	W	S	O	S
K	C	E	O	Z	A	O
I	K	I	C	K	L	C
D	G	R	A	S	S	C
W	O	R	L	D	G	E
K	S	O	C	K	I	R

Word Bank	
world	two
run	grass
soccer	kick
kid	goal

Question and Answer

Directions: Answer the questions about "How to Play Soccer." You may use the words in the Word Bank, below. Note that you will not use all the words in the Word Bank!

1. _____ is called "football" in most places.

2. There are _____ teams in soccer.

3. Soccer is played on the _____ .

4. Players try to _____ the ball.

5. Soccer is played all over the _____ .

Word Bank	
team	world
run	kick
two	eleven
soccer	grass

Fluency Report Card

Directions: Read the article out loud to your teacher. Ask your teacher to time your reading with a watch.

Together, fill out the chart below.

Rate of Reading	Minutes Seconds
Accuracy	Number of Mistakes
Tone	Pitch, Volume, and Rhythm
What You Did Best	Your strengths in fluency!

*Note to Teacher

Rate of Reading: Student should read at a pleasant, conversational pace, not too slowly, and not too quickly.

Accuracy: Student should read with a minimum of mistakes in pronunciation and pauses for punctuation.

Tone: Student should read at a pleasant pitch, with moderate volume, and should vary rhythm as appropriate to each sentence.

102

The Radio Show

Before television, people listened to programs on the radio. Here is a sample script from a radio show.

Host: Welcome to Radio Hour! We have a fun show planned for you today.

Woman: It is brought to you by CoCo's Dog Bones. They are good for your dog's teeth, skin, and coat.

Host: That is right, folks. Now, here is Silly the Clown and his dog, Spot.

Silly: Today, I will tell you a joke. Why did the banana go to the doctor?

Spot: I don't know, Silly.

Silly: Because it was not peeling well!

Spot: I don't think that's a funny joke, Silly.

Silly: Here's another. Spot, what covers the trunk of a tree?

Spot: Bark!

Woman: Well done! When Spot needs a snack, Silly the Clown gives him one of CoCo's Dog Bones. They make Spot look—and sound—his best.

Host: That's all for our show today, folks. Thanks, and don't forget to tune in next week!

Matching

Directions: Study the pictures in the right column. Study the words in the left column. Then, draw a line from each picture to the correct word.

Spot

bone

clown

banana

snack

Fill in the Blanks

Directions: Fill in the blanks with the correct words about The Radio Show. Use words from the word bank below.

1. Radio Hour is brought to you by CoCo's dog _____.

2. Silly has a dog named _____.

3. Silly the _____ likes to tell jokes.

4. A _____ went to the doctor.

5. Spot eats dog bones when he needs a _____.

Word Bank	
snack	clown
banana	bones
Spot	

Color the Words

Directions: Color the picture below. Write the correct word on each line beside the picture.

More on Inflection

Inflection affects the meaning of a sentence.

Directions: Say the sentences below out loud. Stress the word in each sentence that is underlined. Study how the meaning of each sentence changes, depending on which word is stressed.

<u>I</u> don't think that's a funny joke.

(Other people might think it is funny, though.)

I <u>don't</u> think that's a funny joke.

(The listener is offended.)

I don't <u>think</u> that's a funny joke.

(The listener is unsure whether the joke is really funny.)

I don't think <u>that's</u> a funny joke.

(The listener believes that other jokes are funnier.)

I don't think that's a <u>funny</u> joke.

(The listener doesn't find the joke amusing.)

I don't think that's a funny <u>joke</u>.

(The listener believes this is a story rather than a joke.)

More on Emotions

Emotion changes the way a sentence is read.

Directions: Study the sentences below. Read them according to the emotion in parenthesis before each sentence.

(bored)   Welcome to Radio Hour. We have a fun show planned for you today.

(excited)   Welcome to Radio Hour. We have a fun show planned for you today.

(scared)   Welcome to Radio Hour. We have a fun show planned for you today.

(angry)   I'm hungry. Give me a dog bone.

(sad)   I'm hungry. Give me a dog bone.

(eager)   I'm hungry. Give me a dog bone.

(threatening)   Don't forget to tune in next week!

(sleepy)   Don't forget to tune in next week!

(happy)   Don't forget to tune in next week

Readers' Theater

You can read The Radio Show like a play, and even tape record it!

Directions: Choose one person to be the Host. Choose one person to be the Woman. Choose one person to be Silly the Clown. Choose one person to be Spot. Then, act out the radio show below using inflection and emotions.

Host: Welcome to Radio Hour! We have a fun show planned for you today.

Woman: It is brought to you by CoCo's Dog Bones. They are good for your dog's teeth, skin, and coat.

Host: That is right, folks. Now, here is Silly the Clown and his dog, Spot.

Silly: Today, I will tell you a joke. Why did the banana go to the doctor?

Spot: I don't know, Silly.

Silly: Because it was not peeling well!

Spot: I don't think that's a funny joke, Silly.

Silly: Here's another. Spot, what covers the trunk of a tree?

Spot: Bark!

Woman: Well done! When Spot needs a snack, Silly the Clown gives him one of CoCo's Dog Bones. They make Spot look—and sound—his best.

Host: That's all for our show today, folks. Thanks, and don't forget to tune in next week!

Fluency Report Card

Directions: Read the story out loud to your teacher. Ask your teacher to time your reading with a watch.

Together, fill out the chart below.

Rate of Reading	Minutes Seconds
Accuracy	Number of Mistakes
Tone	Pitch, Volume, and Rhythm
What You Did Best	Your strengths in fluency!

*Note to Teacher

Rate of Reading: Student should read at a pleasant, conversational pace, not too slowly, and not too quickly.

Accuracy: Student should read with a minimum of mistakes in pronunciation and pauses for punctuation.

Tone: Student should read at a pleasant pitch, with moderate volume, and should vary rhythm as appropriate to each sentence.

Raptors

A raptor is a bird that hunts with its talons. Talons are like claws. They are sharp. They hold the food while the bird rips it apart with its beak.

Raptors can be hawks or falcons. They can be eagles or osprey. They can be kites or owls.

Raptors are at the top of the food chain. This means they eat small birds and mammals, but no one eats them. Raptors help to control mice and rats. They eat insects. They are helpful birds.

Put up a box in a tree near your house. Then, an owl or small falcon may nest there. Look up in the sky when you are near water. You just might see an osprey or an eagle!

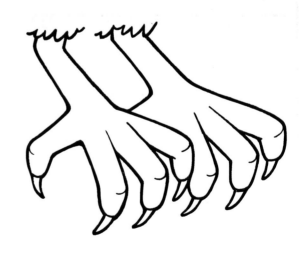

Flash Cards

Note to Teacher: Make double-sided copies, aligning words with the correct pictures so that they appear front-to-back.

Directions: Cut out these flash cards on the lines. Use them to practice fluency before reading "Raptors" on page 111.

beak	talons
nest	hawk
owl	eagle
osprey	kite

Flash Cards *(cont.)*

Matching

Directions: Study the pictures in the column on the right. Study the words in the column on the left. Draw a line to match each picture to the correct word.

eagle

hawk

owl

kite

osprey

nest

Question and Answer

Directions: Use the words from the Word Bank below to complete the sentences.

1. A raptor rips its food apart with its _____.

2. The _____ likes to fly above water.

3. An _____ may move in if you put up a nest box.

4. A _____ is sharp. Raptors use it to hold food.

5. A box makes a good _____ for a falcon or owl.

6. The _____ , the owl, and the eagle are all raptors.

Word Bank	
owl	beak
talon	hawk
eagle	nest

Stressed and Unstressed Syllables

Directions: Read the sentences below out loud. Put a "\" mark above the syllables that are stressed. Put a "–" mark above the syllables that are unstressed. The first one has been done for you.

Note: You may want to clap as you read each sentence, to hear the rhythm.

```
  –   \   –     \    –   –   \   –
```
1. A raptor hunts with its talons.

2. Talons hold a raptor's food.

3. Raptors can be eagles or osprey.

4. Owls eat mammals and insects.

5. You can put up a nest box near your house.

Which is Which?

Directions: Color the picture of the raptor below. Write in the correct word in the blank lines to identify each object.

Fluency Report Card

Directions: Read the story out loud to your teacher. Ask your teacher to time your reading with a watch.

Together, fill out the chart below.

Rate of Reading	Minutes Seconds
Accuracy	Number of Mistakes
Tone	Pitch, Volume, and Rhythm
What You Did Best	Your strengths in fluency!

*Note to Teacher

Rate of Reading: Student should read at a pleasant, conversational pace, not too slowly, and not too quickly.

Accuracy: Student should read with a minimum of mistakes in pronunciation and pauses for punctuation.

Tone: Student should read at a pleasant pitch, with moderate volume, and should vary rhythm as appropriate to each sentence.

Riddles

Riddle #1

Question: What does a house wear?

Answer: A-dress!

Riddle #2

Question: Why did the belt get put in jail?

Answer: For holding up the pants!

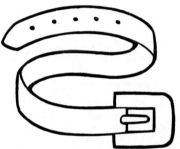

Riddle #3

Question: What did one chip say to the other?

Answer: Let's go for a dip!

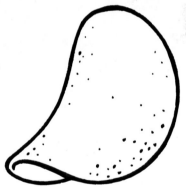

Riddle #4

Question: What did the sock say to the foot?

Answer: You're putting me on!

Matching

Directions: Look at the pictures on this page. Draw a line from each picture to the correct word at the bottom.

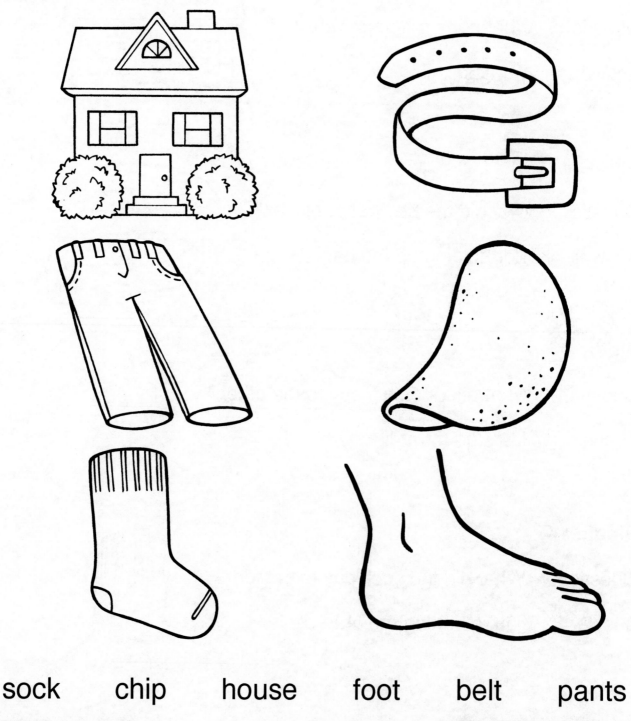

sock   chip   house   foot   belt   pants

Question or Exclamation?

Remember that a question mark looks like this: _?_

An exclamation point looks like this: _!_

Directions: Write a question mark after each question below.

Write an exclamation point after each exclamation below.

1. Why did the belt get put in jail ____

2. For holding up the pants ____

3. What did the sock say to the foot ____

4. You're putting me on ____

5. What does a house wear ____

6. A-dress ____

7. What did one chip say to the other ____

8. Let's go for a dip ____

Word Bingo

Directions: Play Bingo, using words from "Riddles."

Copy the words below onto individual file cards or small pieces of paper. Choose one person to be the Caller. The Caller begins by choosing one word to call out. Each player then marks the square on his or her game card which contains that word.

Players may use markers in the form of dried beans, pennies, or small pebbles. You may want to play so that the first person to mark off an entire row across, down, or diagonally wins. Alternatively, you might want to play until every word has been called and marked.

Word Bingo *(cont.)*

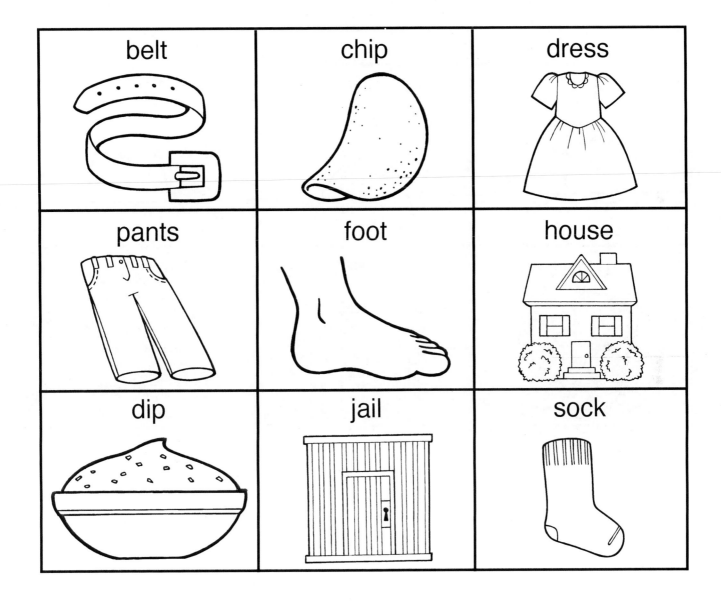

belt	chip	dress
pants	foot	house
dip	jail	sock

Word Bingo *(cont.)*

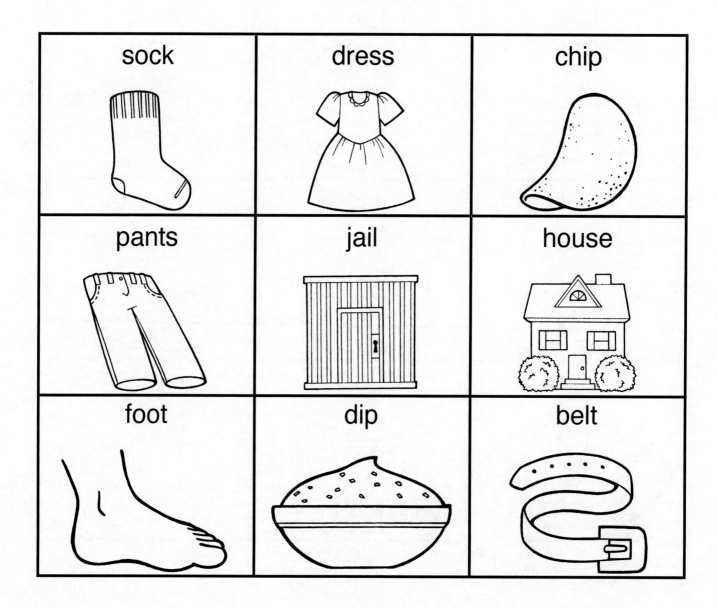

sock	dress	chip
pants	jail	house
foot	dip	belt

Word Bingo *(cont.)*

jail	dip	sock
belt	pants	foot
house	dress	chip

Fluency Report Card

Directions: Read the story out loud to your teacher. Ask your teacher to time your reading with a watch.

Together, fill out the chart below.

Rate of Reading	Minutes Seconds
Accuracy	Number of Mistakes
Tone	Pitch, Volume, and Rhythm
What You Did Best	Your strengths in fluency!

*Note to Teacher

Rate of Reading: Student should read at a pleasant, conversational pace, not too slowly, and not too quickly.

Accuracy: Student should read with a minimum of mistakes in pronunciation and pauses for punctuation.

Tone: Student should read at a pleasant pitch, with moderate volume, and should vary rhythm as appropriate to each sentence.

The Game Show

Choose one student to read each part in this game show below.

Host: Welcome to "What's the Question!" Today, we meet Lyn, Jon, and Pat. They'll try to answer each question first. Let's get started. Is everybody ready?

All: Yes!

Host: What did the chewing gum say to the shoe?

Lyn: Go away?

Jon: Don't step on me!

Pat: I'm stuck on you!

Host: Pat is correct! Next question: Why do birds fly south?

Pat: This is a tough one.

Lyn: I'm not sure!

Jon: Because it's too far to walk!

Host: Well done, Jon. Last question: Why don't Teddy Bears need to eat?

Jon: They've already eaten?

Pat: They're just toys?

Lyn: I know! Because they're already stuffed.

Host: Good job, Lyn! It looks like we have a tie. You'll each get a prize. Thanks for playing!

Pictures and Words

Directions: Study the pictures below. Then, write the correct word below each picture.

Crossword

Directions: Write the correct answer in each blank. Then, fill in the crossword.

Across

3. Her teddy _____ is stuffed.

4. He won first _____ for reading.

5. I can _____ to school.

6. We like to play with _____ .

7. Don't chew _____ in class.

8. Do you hear the _____ singing?

9. Birds _____ south.

Down

1. The dog _____ his shoe.

2. I like to _____ apples.

Read for Character

Directions: You can create a real character when you read, just by adding emotion. Read The Game Show out loud, following the description of each character below.

Character	Emotion
Host	excited
Lyn	gloomy
Jon	nervous
Pat	bored

Host: Welcome to "What's the Question!" Today, we meet Lyn, Jon, and Pat. They'll try to answer each question first. Let's get started. Is everybody ready?

All: Yes!

Host: What did the chewing gum say to the shoe?

Lyn: Go away?

Jon: Don't step on me!

Pat: I'm stuck on you!

Host: Pat is correct! Next question: Why do birds fly south?

Pat: This is a tough one.

Lyn: I'm not sure!

Jon: Because it's too far to walk!

Host: Well done, Jon. Last question: Why don't Teddy Bears need to eat?

Jon: They've already eaten?

Pat: They're just toys?

Lyn: I know! Because they're already stuffed.

Host: Good job, Lyn! It looks like we have a tie. You'll all get a prize. Thanks for playing!

Contractions

Directions: A contraction is one word which is formed by joining two words with an apostrophe. Here is a list of words below. Read them out loud. Then, read the contraction.

what	+	is	=	what's
they	+	will	=	they'll
let	+	us	=	let's
do	+	not	=	don't
I	+	am	=	I'm
you	+	all	=	you'll

More on Contractions

It's your turn to make contractions.

Directions: Look at the words in Box 1. Look at the words in Box 2. Put them together with an apostrophe to form as many contractions as possible in Box 3. You should be able to make seven contractions.

Box 1
let
do
what
you
I
they

Box 2
us
is
all
will
not
am

Box 3
1.
2.
3.
4.
5.
6.
7.

Apostrophes

An apostrophe is used in a contraction to take the place of a missing letter. It looks like this: _'_ .

Directions: Below, study each word. Put an apostrophe in the correct place. Then, write the missing letter or letters on the line to the right. Write the contraction again on the next line. The first one has been done for you.

1. d o n ' t   _____o_____   _____don't_____

2. y o u l l   _____   _____

3. I m   _____   _____

4. t h e y l l   _____   _____

5. w h a t s   _____   _____

6. l e t s   _____   _____

Fluency Report Card

Directions: Read the story out loud to your teacher. Ask your teacher to time your reading with a watch.

Together, fill out the chart below.

Rate of Reading	Minutes Seconds
Accuracy	Number of Mistakes
Tone	Pitch, Volume, and Rhythm
What You Did Best	Your strengths in fluency!

*Note to Teacher

Rate of Reading: Student should read at a pleasant, conversational pace, not too slowly, and not too quickly.

Accuracy: Student should read with a minimum of mistakes in pronunciation and pauses for punctuation.

Tone: Student should read at a pleasant pitch, with moderate volume, and should vary rhythm as appropriate to each sentence.

Tongue Twisters

Students may practice these classic tongue twisters below and on the next page for a fun method of increasing fluency.

Point out that tongue twisters rely on alliteration—the repetition of particular sounds within a sentence.

- She sells sea shells on the sea shore.

- A proper cup of coffee from a copper coffee pot.

- The Big Book Crook took the big cookbook.

- How much wood could a wood chuck chuck, if a wood chuck could chuck wood?

- Peter Piper picked a peck of pickled peppers, a peck of pickled peppers Peter Piper picked.

If Peter Piper picked a peck of pickled peppers, where's the peck of pickled peppers Peter Piper picked?

Tongue Twisters (cont.)

- A skunk sat on a stump.

  The skunk thunk the stump stunk,

  But the stump thunk the skunk stunk.

- A tutor who tooted the flute

  Tried to tutor two tooters to toot.

  Said the two to the tutor:

  "Is it harder to toot or

  To tutor two tooters to toot?"

Award for Rate of Reading

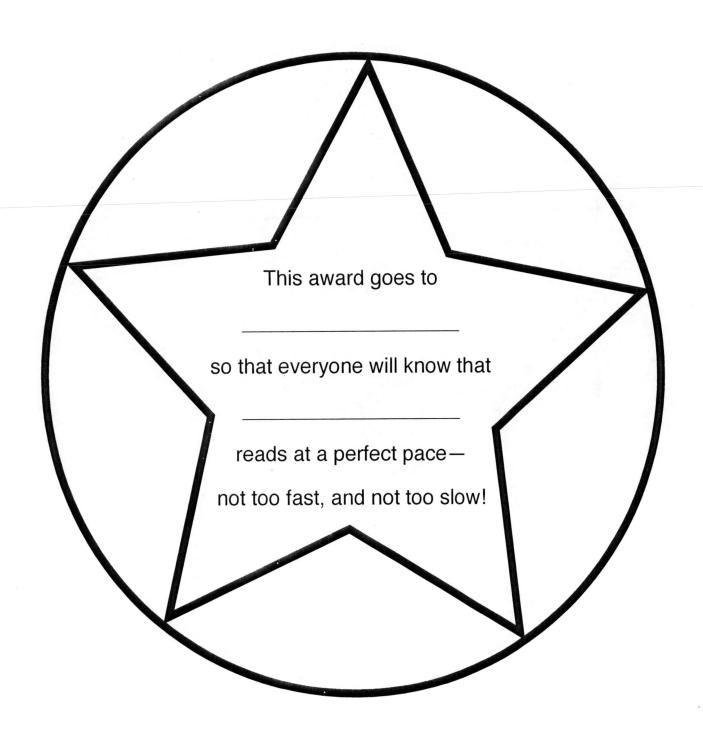

This award goes to

_____

so that everyone will know that

_____

reads at a perfect pace—

not too fast, and not too slow!

Award for Accuracy

For reading every word
with skill and accuracy—

with sharp eyes and good
pronunciation, too—

_____

receives this prize!

Award for Tone

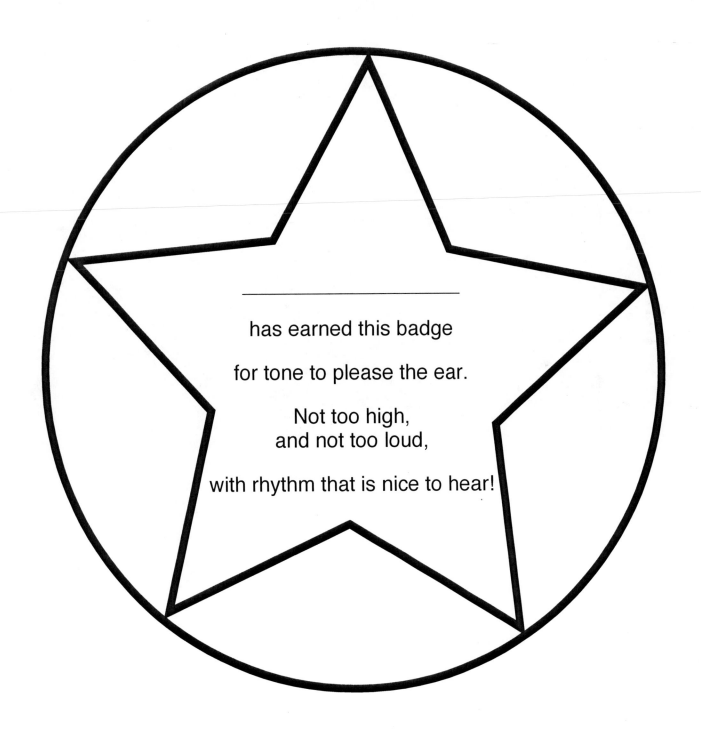

_____

has earned this badge

for tone to please the ear.

Not too high,
and not too loud,

with rhythm that is nice to hear!

Answer Key

Page 13

Sam was a <u>dog</u>. He was big and brown. He loved to play with a <u>green</u> ball.

One day, Sam lost his ball. He was sad.

He found a toy in the kitchen. "No. That is an egg Sam," said the <u>girl</u>.

Sam found a toy in the bedroom. "No. That is a <u>shoe</u>, Sam," said the boy.

Then they gave him a new green <u>ball</u>. Sam played and <u>played</u>. Now he was happy.

Page 21

1. Meg
2. lake
3. wind
4. sick
5. ride

Page 26

2. one syllable
3. two syllables
4. one syllable
5. one syllable
6. two syllables

page 28

2. (han) - dy
3. (mu) - sic
4. (ri) - ding
5. (fea) - ther

Page 29

2. po - (ny)
3. dan - (dy)
4. Yan - (kee)
5. ma - (ca) - ro - (ni)

Page 36

2. He sat in a golden valley, ☺ and he looked lost and sad.
3. I called to the dog to come to me, ☺ but he just sat still.
4. "Spot!" I said, ☺ Then, the dog ran to me and barked.
5. Now, a little girl walked up, ☺ "There you are, Spot!" she said.
6. The dog jumped up on the girl and licked her face. ☺ "I thought he was lost," she told me.

Page 37

1. highway
2. forest
3. island
4. valley
5. water
6. sky

Page 41

1. owning
2. friendly
3. playful
4. softly
5. healthy

Page 42

playful
healthy
softly
softer
player
playing
played
owner
owned
owning
friendly
healthful

Answer Key *(cont.)*

Page 45

Accept all reasonable sentences that use the given nouns, root words, and suffixes.

Page 48

1. beside
2. discover
3. underground
4. replace
5. transform

Page 49

A tree is a plant. It has a trunk and leaves. It has branches and twigs. Trees have roots <u>underground</u>.

Trees <u>replace</u> bad air with good air. People need air to breathe. This is one reason to love trees.

Trees also give us shade. It is nice to sit <u>beside</u> a tree in the sun. Trees keep us cool.

Some trees give us fruit. People pick it off trees. Trees <u>transform</u> our world.

It is good to plant a tree. Find some land. Dig a hole. Cover the tree roots with dirt. <u>Discover</u> the joy of trees!

Page 53

1. roots
2. discover
3. beside
4. replace
5. tree

Page 57

1. ate
2. throws
3. Chew
4. licked
5. chew

Page 58

A	D	F	K	G	L	E
P	L	A	T	T	E	R
W	Q	M	W	Z	E	P
Q	S	B	C	A	A	Y
U	D	E	B	L	T	U
E	C	B	O	N	E	C
E	J	A	N	X	K	S
N	L	I	C	K	E	D
C	A	T	H	C	P	G

Page 59

Jack Sprat could eat no fat <u>.</u>

His wife could eat no lean <u>.</u>

And so between the two of them,

They licked the platter clean <u>.</u>

Jack ate all the lean <u>.</u>

The queen ate all the fat <u>.</u>

The bone they chewed it clean,

Then threw it to the cat <u>.</u>

Page 65

man, sack

seven, I

wife, cat

kit, walk

Page 66

22

Page 67

Saint Ives

As I was going to Saint Ives <u>,</u>

I met a man with seven wives.

Each wife had seven sacks <u>,</u>

Each sack had seven cats <u>,</u>

Answer Key (cont.)

Each cat had seven kits.

Kits , cats , sacks , and wives ,

How many were going to Saint Ives?

Page 68

1. The man, his <u>wife,</u> and his <u>cat</u> went to Saint Ives.
2. I put the cat in a <u>sack,</u> called to my <u>wife,</u> and went for a <u>walk.</u>
3. <u>I</u> walked <u>seven</u> days, then found my lost <u>cat.</u> (or <u>wife</u>).
4. My <u>wife</u> pets her <u>cat,</u> but it bites.
5. The <u>man,</u> the <u>wife,</u> and the <u>cat</u> took a walk.

Page 69

Across

3. Her <u>cats</u> had baby kits.
5. His <u>wife</u> owns seven cats.
6. The <u>man</u> could not find his sack.

Down

1. The man and his wife went for a <u>walk.</u>
2. Each wife had <u>seven</u> cats.
4. I put my bone in an empty <u>sack.</u>

Page 74

1. cow
2. you
3. play
4. horse
5. Write

Page 75

Accept all reasonable answers from the choices given.

Page 76

1. He likes rats<u>.</u>
2. How are you<u>?</u>
3. The rat is white<u>.</u>
4. Do you like cows <u>?</u>
5. Who likes school <u>?</u>
6. Jo owns a horse <u>.</u>

Page 77

Grade for content, as well as for names, date, greeting, and closing.

Page 81

1. Dad
2. Bill and Katy
3. friends
4. a dollar
5. I'm sorry.

Page 93

1. Laugh, Kookaburra <u>!</u>
2. Where is the tree <u>?</u>
3. Stop eating so much <u>!</u>
4. Who likes gumdrops <u>?</u>
5. Look at that bird <u>!</u>

Page 100

W	E	E	T	C	G	Y
R	U	N	W	S	O	S
K	C	E	O	Z	A	O
I	K	I	C	K	L	C
D	G	R	A	S	S	C
W	O	R	L	D	G	E
K	S	O	C	K	I	R

Page 101

1. Soccer
2. two
3. grass
4. kick
5. world